How to Thrive on a Shoestring:
Real-Life Strategies for Budget Success

By

Virginia Pitts

Copyright © by Virginia Pitts 2024. All rights reserved.

Before this document is duplicated or reproduced in any manner, the publisher's consent must be gained. Therefore, the contents within can neither be stored electronically, transferred, nor kept in a database. Neither in Part nor full can the document be copied, scanned, faxed, or retained without approval from the publisher or creator.

Table of Contents

INTRODUCTION 15

    The Art of Living Well When Your Purse Strings Are Tight 15

Chapter 1: Creating a Budget Blueprint and Assessing Your Financial Situation. 19

    Understanding the importance of assessment. 19

    Taking Inventory: Income and Expense 20

    Evaluating assets and liabilities 21

    Defining financial goals 22

    Embracing the Power of Assessment 22

Chapter 1: Creating a Budget Blueprint: Setting Financial Goals 24

    The Benefits of Setting Financial Goals 24

    Understanding the many types of financial goals. 26

    Short-term Goals 26

    Medium-term Goals 26

    Long-Term Goals 27

    The S.M.A.R.T. Method for Goal Setting 27

    Specific 28

    Measurable 28

    Achievable 28

    Relevant 29

Time-bound.. 29

The Value of Prioritizing Goals................................... 30

Creating a goal hierarchy. 30

Breaking your goals into actionable steps. 30

Staying flexible and adaptable 31

Celebrating Milestones and Progress........................ 32

Conclusion: Empowerment through Goal Setting. 32

Chapter 2. Mastering Money Management: Tracking Expenses and Income 33

Importance of Tracking Expenses and Income 33

Practical Strategies for Tracking Expenses and Income. 34

    1. Choose your tracking method. 34

    2. Record each transaction. 35

    3. Categorize your expenses. 35

    4. Review and analyze your spending patterns. 36

    5. Create realistic budgets and goals. 36

Overcoming Common Pitfalls. 37

    1. Lack of consistency... 37

    2. Difficulty categorizing expenses. 38

    3. Overcome Tracking Fatigue.............................. 38

Leveraging Technology for Enhanced Tracking 39

Conclusion: Empowerment through the tracking of expenses and income. 40

Chapter 2: Developing Smart Spending Habits. 41

The Essence of Smart Spending. 41

Strategies for Smart Spending. 42

    2. Differentiate between needs and wants. 42

    3. Practice delayed gratification. 43

    4. Comparison Shop 43

    5. Set spending limits. 43

    6. Embrace minimalism. 44

Overcoming Common Challenges. 44

    1. Peer Pressure 45

    2. Emotional Spending. 45

    3. Lifestyle Inflation 46

    4. Impulse purchases. 46

Leveraging Rewards and Incentives. 47

Conclusion: A Journey Toward Financial 47

Freedom 47

Chapter 2: Strategies for Saving and Cutting Costs ... 49

The Significance of Saving and Cutting Costs 49

Strategies to Save More 50

    1. Pay Yourself First. 50

    2. Set specific savings goals. 51

Real-Life Strategies for Budget Success

    3. Automate your savings. 51

    4. Reduce unnecessary expenses. 52

    5. Take advantage of windfalls and bonuses. 52

    1. Reduce housing expenses. 53

    2. Lower utility bills. 53

    3. Reduce Transportation Costs. 54

    4. Shop Smart. 54

    5. Reduce Dining and Entertainment Expenses. 55

Overcoming Common Challenges 55

    1. Lifestyle Inflation 56

    2. Peer Pressure 56

    3. Emotional Spending 57

    4. Lack of financial literacy 57

Conclusion: A Path to Financial Freedom. 58

Chapter: Maximizing Income Potential; Exploring Additional Income Streams 59

The Power of Multiple Income Streams 59

Strategies for Exploring Additional Income Streams ... 60

    1. Identify Your Skills and Interests 60

    2. Explore Freelancing and Consulting 60

    3. Start a Side Business 61

    4. Invest in Real Estate 61

    5. Invest in Dividend-Paying Stocks 62

- 6. Explore Affiliate Marketing 62
- Overcoming Common Challenges 63
  - 1. Time Management 63
  - 2. Skill Development... 63
  - 3. Financial Risk 64
  - 4. Market Saturation 64
- Conclusion: Unlocking Your Income Potential........... 65

Chapter 3: Maximizing Income Potential................... 66
- The Significance of Maximizing Income Potential 66
- Strategies for Maximizing Income Potential............... 67
  - 1. Invest in Education and Skill Development 67
  - 2. Pursue Career Advancement Opportunities....... 67
  - 3. Explore Side Hustles and Freelancing 68
  - 4. Negotiate Your Salary and Benefits 69
  - 5. Monetize Your Passions and Hobbies.................... 69
- Overcoming Encounters 70
  - 1. Lack of Confidence 70
  - 2. Time Constraints 71
  - 3. Fear of Failure 71
- Challenge: 72
  - 4. Financial Constraints 72
- Conclusion: Embracing the Journey to Financial Empowerment... 73

Chapter 3: Making the Most of Your Resources 74
    The Value of Resourcefulness 74
    Strategies for Making the Most of Your Resources 75
        1. Budgeting and Financial Planning 75
    Challenge: 75
        2. Time Management 76
    Task: 76
        3. Skill Development and Learning 76
    Task: 77
        4. Networking and Relationship Building 77
        Daily Test: 78
        5. Creativity & Innovation 78
    Daily Challenge Tasks: 78
    Overcoming Common Challenges 79
        1. Procrastination and Inertia 79
        2. Lack of Focus and Distractions 80
    Daily Challenge Tasks: 80
        3. Fear of failure and perfectionism 80
        4. Lack of Support and Accountability 81
    Conclusion: Empowering Yourself to Thrive 81

Chapter 4: Navigating Debt; Understanding Different Types of Debt 82
    The Importance of Understanding Debt 82

Understanding the Different Types of Debt 83

    1. Good Debt. 83

Daily Challenge Tasks: 84

    2. Bad Debt.. 84

Daily Challenge Tasks: 85

Chapter 4: Establishing a Debt Repayment Plan 86

The Importance of Creating a Debt Payment Plan 86

    Step 1: Take Inventory of Your Debt 87

    Step 2: Set your goals. 87

    Step 3: Select a Repayment Strategy..................... 87

    Step 4: Set a Budget 88

    Step 5: Track Your Progress 89

    Step 6: Stay Motivated 89

Daily Challenge Task: 89

Chapter 4: Avoiding Common Debt Traps.................. 90

Understanding Common Debt Traps. 90

    1. Credit card debt. 90

    2. Payday Loans 91

    3. Rent-to-Own Stores 91

    4: Buy Now, Pay Later Services 92

Practical Strategies to Avoid Debt Traps.................... 92

    1. Create an Emergency Fund.............................. 92

    Daily Challenge Task:... 93

Real-Life Strategies for Budget Success

2. Keep to a Budget 93

3. Avoid high-interest debt. 93

Daily Challenge Task 94

4. Read the fine print 94

Trial Challenge: 94

5. Practice Delayed Gratification. 95

Daily Challenge 95

Conclusion: Empowering Yourself to Avoid Debt Traps.
.... 96

Chapter 5: Thriving in Daily Life: Budget-Friendly Meal Planning and Cooking Tips. 97

The Benefits of Budget-Friendly Meal Planning 97

The Personal Touch: My Journey with Cost-Effective Meal Planning 98

Strategies for Budget-Friendly Meal Planning 99

    Daily Challenge 99

    2. Plan your meals. 100

    3. Shop Smart. 100

    Daily Challenge 101

    4. Embrace Batch Cooking. 101

    Daily Challenge 101

    5. Be Creative with Leftovers 101

    Daily Challenge Task 102

Conclusion: Empowering Yourself to Thrive on a Budget. 102

Chapter 5: Affordable Transportation Solutions 103

The importance of affordable transportation........... 103

Personal Journey: Achieving Financial Freedom with Affordable Transportation...................... 104

Practical Tips for Cost-Effective Transportation Solutions 105

    1. Investigate other modes of transportation. 105

Daily Challenge Test:........................ 105

    2. Carpooling and Ridesharing 106

    3. Utilize public transportation. 106

    Daily Task: 107

    4. Optimize Your Vehicle's Use 107

    Challenge: 107

    5. Embrace Active Transportation 108

    Daily Challenge Tasks: 108

Conclusion: Empowering Yourself With Affordable Transportation 108

Chapter 5: Find Free and Low-Cost Entertainment Options 110

The Benefits of Free and Low-Cost Entertainment ... 110

Personal Reflection: My Path to Embracing Low-Cost Entertainment 111

Real-Life Strategies for Budget Success

How to Find Free and Low-Cost Entertainment Options 112

    1. Explore your community. 112

    2. Take advantage of nature. 112

    Daily Challenge Tasks: 113

    3. Host social gatherings 113

    4. Get creative with DIY projects. 113

    5. Make Use of Free Online Resources 114

    Daily Challenge Tasks: 114

Conclusion: Enjoying the Benefits of Low-Cost Entertainment 114

Chapter 6: Planning for the Future and Investing Wisely for Long-Term Financial Stability 115

Understanding the Value of Investing..................... 115

Personal Reflection: My Journey to Invest Wisely 116

How to Invest Wisely for Long-Term Financial Stability 117

    1. Start early and be consistent. 117

    Daily Test: 117

    2. Diversify your investments. 118

    Daily Challenge Tasks: 118

    3. Invest for the long term. 118

    Diurnal Challenge Tasks:................................... 119

    4. Take advantage of tax-advantaged accounts. ... 119

Challenge: 120

5. Stay informed and educated. 120

Conclusion: Gaining Control of Your Financial Future Through Wise Investing 121

Chapter 6: Planning for the Future; Budgeting for Retirement. 122

The Value of Planning for Retirement 122

Practical Strategies for Budget-Friendly Retirement. 123

1. Start early and make saving a priority: 123

2. Take advantage of employer-sponsored retirement plans: 123

Daily Challenge Tasks: 124

3. Investigate Other Retirement Savings Options: 124

Daily Challenge Tasks: 125

4. Cut back on expenses and live below your means: 125

5. Stay informed and educated about retirement planning. 126

Test: 126

Conclusion: Gaining Control Over Your Retirement Future 127

Conclusion: Embracing the Shoestring Lifestyle for Long-Term Financial Freedom 128

1. Mindset Matters 129

Real-Life Strategies for Budget Success

2. Little moves Lead to Big Results 129

3. Embrace Creativity and Resourcefulness 130

4. Community and Support 130

5. Celebrate Your Successes 130

INTRODUCTION

The Art of Living Well When Your Purse Strings Are Tight

In a society where materialism's glitz and glamour frequently take centre stage, there is a quieter, more tenacious force at work: the skill of living well on a shoestring. Consider this: a lovely apartment filled with thrifted treasures, a table set with a simple yet delicious prepared supper, and a family gathering around to share stories and laughs. This isn't a scenario from a glossy magazine or a planned Instagram post; it's a glimpse into the daily lives of millions who have perfected the delicate dance of extending a dollar without compromising joy or fulfilment.

But first, let's go back to the beginning, when the idea of living on a budget may have seemed difficult or even disappointing. Consider a young couple who recently graduated from college, full of goals and aspirations but burdened by student loans and entry-level jobs. That was my husband and me, embarking on our adventure into adulthood with nothing except enthusiasm and a small savings account.

Real-Life Strategies for Budget Success

As we settled into our first apartment, a cozy but confined place that served as both our living room, dining room, and bedroom, we understood that our goals of financial independence would take more than just wishful thinking. We needed to roll up our sleeves, tighten our belts, and face the challenge of living within our means. And so began our crash lesson in the art of living on a shoestring.

At first, the road ahead appeared intimidating, full of difficulties and unknowns. With our limited earnings, how could we afford groceries, let alone save for the future? Will we ever be able to enjoy the comforts that seemed so far out of reach? But, as we quickly realized, necessity truly is the mother of invention, and our drive to make ends meet revealed a treasure mine of inventive solutions and creativity we had no idea we possessed.

Our trip wasn't without challenges and sacrifices. There were days when our bank account was dangerously close to zero and nights when we only ate a dish of pasta. But, despite it all, we held onto a shared notion that living well did not imply living lavishly—that true happiness might be found not in the accumulation of stuff, but in the richness of experience and connection.

So, armed with little more than drive and a willingness to adapt, we set out to carve our own route to financial independence. We investigated charity stores for hidden treasures and learnt how w to repair and repurpose objects that others would reject. We traded costly nights out for relaxing evenings at home, complete with cooked food and board games. And with each modest victory—a debt repaid, a savings goal met—we felt a renewed sense of empowerment and purpose.

But our path was more than just squeezing pennies and counting cents; it was a journey of self-discovery and development. We learnt vital things along the road, including the true meaning of abundance and the power of thankfulness. We learnt that the simple pleasures of life—a warm embrace, a shared laugh, a stunning sunset—are what provide happiness, not the amassing of wealth.

As time passed and our circumstances changed, so did our approach to budgeting and financial management. We discovered new ways to boost our income while decreasing our expenses, using our abilities and hobbies to generate extra cash streams. We invested in our future by creating a nest egg that would bring security and peace of mind in the years ahead.

And now, as we reflect on our transition from struggling newlyweds to financially affluent grownups, we are struck with great appreciation and humility. We are appreciative of the lessons learnt, obstacles faced, and growth that have resulted from adopting the shoestring lifestyle. And it is with that same attitude of appreciation and humility that we present this book—a road map for those who, like us, are ready to embark on their own path to financial independence.

Real-Life Strategies for Budget Success

So, whether you're a recent graduate saddled with school debt, a single mom struggling to make ends meet, or simply someone looking for a simpler, more meaningful way of life, know that you're not alone. The road to financial freedom may be long and winding, but with determination, inventiveness, and a willingness to embrace the shoestring lifestyle, it is not only attainable but also immensely satisfying. So, join me, my reader, on a voyage of exploration, empowerment, and, finally, transformation.

Chapter 1: Creating a Budget Blueprint and Assessing Your Financial Situation.

In the enormous terrain of personal money, creating a budget is the foundation of financial stability and success. Much like a professional architect methodically designs every component of a building before laying the foundation, constructing a budget takes thorough assessment, thoughtful planning, and a clear understanding of one's financial situation. In this chapter, we'll go over how to create a budget blueprint by first examining your financial status.

Understanding the importance of assessment.

Consider embarking on a cruise without a map or compass, crossing the perilous waters of uncertainty. Such is the treacherous voyage of managing funds without a clear picture of one's financial status. Assessment serves as a guiding light, illuminating the route ahead and providing essential insights into where you are and where you want to go.

Real-Life Strategies for Budget Success

Assessing your financial condition entails a thorough evaluation of all elements of your finances, including income, expenses, assets, liabilities, and financial objectives. It's similar to taking a snapshot of your present financial situation—a candid assessment of your financial health, strengths, and places for development.

Taking Inventory: Income and Expense

At the heart of financial assessment is a study of revenue and expenses—the lifeblood of your financial system. Income is the amount of money that enters your account, whether it comes from your principal work, a side hustle, investments, or another source. Understanding your income sources provides insight into your earning potential and prospective areas for expansion.

On the other hand, expenses signify money outflow—every dollar spent helps to shape your financial reality. Every expenditure, from set expenses like rent or mortgage payments to variable expenses like groceries, utilities, and entertainment, has an impact on your financial picture. By rigorously documenting your expenses, you receive useful insights into your spending habits and can identify areas where changes may be required to fit with your financial goals.

Evaluating assets and liabilities

Beyond income and expenses, there is a more in-depth study of assets and liabilities, which are the foundation of your net worth. Assets are anything you own that has monetary value, including cash and savings accounts, investments, real estate, and personal property. Liabilities, on the other hand, are your financial commitments, such as debts, loans, and outstanding payments.

Assessing your assets and liabilities gives you a complete picture of your financial situation, allowing you to compute your net worth (the difference between your total assets and liabilities). A positive net worth indicates financial health and stability, as your assets surpass your liabilities. In contrast, a negative net worth indicates possible financial difficulties, identifying prospects for debt reduction and wealth growth.

Defining financial goals

No evaluation of your financial status is complete without a clear statement of your financial objectives—the guiding lights that illuminate your road to wealth. Whether your goals are debt repayment, savings, investments, housing, education, or retirement, identifying them precisely is critical to creating a budget design that corresponds with your objectives.

Financial goals serve as the North Star, guiding your financial decisions and activities while also motivating and directing you on your path to financial freedom. Setting SMART goals—Specific, Measurable, Achievable, Relevant, and Time-bound—provides a road map for achievement, breaking down high goals into achievable actions and milestones.

Embracing the Power of Assessment

In the area of personal finance, information is power, and assessment is the foundation of educated decision-making. By having a thorough awareness of your financial condition, including income, expenses, assets, liabilities, and aspirations, you empower yourself to take control of your financial future.

Assessment lays the framework for creating a budget blueprint that matches your beliefs, priorities, and goals, allowing you to make clear and purposeful financial decisions and actions. Whether you're looking to pay off debt, save money, or achieve financial independence, the first step is to assess where you are now and where you want to go.

In the next chapters, we'll go deeper into the process of developing a budget blueprint, discussing tactics for generating a realistic budget, defining financial objectives, and navigating the complexity of money management. But, before we begin that journey, take the time to examine your financial situation—a little but significant step toward financial empowerment and wealth.

Real-Life Strategies for Budget Success

Chapter 1: Creating a Budget Blueprint: Setting Financial Goals

Setting financial objectives acts as the conductor in the personal finance symphony, directing our activities and decisions toward a harmonious and profitable future. Financial goals, like a compass pointing north, provide direction, purpose, and inspiration as we strive for financial stability and success. In this chapter, we'll look at the process of defining financial objectives, which combines vision, intention, and pragmatism to develop a road map for reaching our dreams.

The Benefits of Setting Financial Goals

Imagine you're at the helm of a ship, navigating a route across unfamiliar waters to a far horizon. Setting financial objectives is similar to mapping a course: it provides us with a destination to aim for as well as a sense of purpose and direction. Whether your goals are to pay off debt, save for a down payment on a house, develop an emergency fund, or retire early, they provide a road map for making dreams a reality.

Growing up in a modest environment, I learnt the importance of hard work and cautious financial management at a young age. Money was always tight, but my parents instilled in me the value of setting goals and working hard to achieve them.

One of my earliest memories of goal setting is from my teenage years. I had set my sights on entering college, but with tuition fees skyrocketing and my family's limited financial resources, the notion appeared intimidating. Determined to achieve my aspirations, I made a goal of allocating a portion of my earnings from part-time employment and summer gigs to my education fund.

Each salary served as a stepping stone toward my objective, and every dollar saved moved me closer to achieving my ambition of pursuing further education. It wasn't easy—there were temptations along the road, including impulse purchases and peer pressure—but my steadfast dedication to my objective kept me focused and motivated.

Fast forward to my senior year of high school, and I had a large sum in my college fund—a monument to the power of setting specific, achievable objectives and working hard to achieve them. Thanks to my savings and a combination of scholarships, grants, and student loans, I was able to attend college without putting a substantial financial strain on myself or my family.

Understanding the many types of financial goals.

Financial objectives come in different shapes and sizes, and each serves a distinct role in our quest for financial well-being. Financial goals are broadly divided into three categories: short-term, medium-term, and long-term.

Short-term Goals

Short-term goals are those that you want to achieve in the next year or two. Paying off a credit card balance, saving for a vacation, or purchasing a new appliance are examples of smaller-scale and more immediate goals. Short-term goals provide fast victories and real rewards, which keep you motivated as you work toward greater goals.

Medium-term Goals

Medium-term goals span two to five years and sometimes demand more planning and commitment to achieve. Examples include saving for a down payment on a house, purchasing a car, or funding a wedding or large vacation. Medium-term goals necessitate a combination of patience and perseverance as you work steadily toward them over time.

Long-Term Goals

Long-term goals are those that you want to complete in five years or more. These objectives frequently necessitate extensive planning, devotion, and tenacity, as well as a willingness to forego immediate enjoyment in favor of long-term benefits. Long-term goals can include saving for retirement, supporting a child's education, or achieving financial independence.

The S.M.A.R.T. Method for Goal Setting

When it comes to establishing financial objectives, the SMART approach is your best friend. Specific, Measurable, Achievable, Relevant, and Time-bound (SMART) is a framework for defining clear, practical, and realistic goals.

Specific

A precise goal is clearly stated. Instead of saying, "I want to save money," specify how much you want to save and what you're saving for. For instance, "I want to save $5,000 for a down payment on a house within the next two years."

Measurable

A measurable aim is one that can be tracked and quantified. It's critical to be able to track your progress toward your goals so you know when you've accomplished them. Using the example above, you may track your progress by checking your savings account balance every month to ensure you're on schedule to reach $5,000 in two years.

Achievable

An achievable aim is one that is both attainable and practical in light of your existing circumstances. While it is vital to dream large, it is also important to create attainable goals. Consider your income, expenses, and saving habits while setting goals to ensure they are attainable.

Relevant

A relevant aim is one that is in line with your values, priorities, and long-term aspirations. Before setting a goal, consider why it is important to you and how it fits into your overall financial strategy. If a goal does not correspond to your values or priorities, it may not be worth pursuing.

Time-bound

A time-bound goal has a set deadline or timetable for completion. Setting a deadline creates a sense of urgency and accountability, which motivates you to take action and stay focused on your objective. Set reasonable deadlines that give you adequate time to complete your goal without feeling overwhelmed.

Real-Life Strategies for Budget Success

The Value of Prioritizing Goals

With so many financial goals competing for our attention, it's critical to prioritize them according to their relevance and urgency. Not all goals are created equal, and some may necessitate more time, effort, and resources to complete than others. Prioritizing your objectives allows you to focus your energy and resources on the ones that are most important to you, ensuring that you make consistent progress toward accomplishing them.

Creating a goal hierarchy.

A goal hierarchy, or prioritized list of goals based on their relative relevance and urgency, is one method for prioritizing your goals. Begin by determining your most essential and urgent goals, like as paying off high-interest debt or establishing an emergency fund. Then, work your way down the list, giving each goal a priority rating based on its importance to your overall financial plan.

Breaking your goals into actionable steps.

After you've identified and prioritized your goals, it's time to turn them into concrete steps. Consider each objective to be a puzzle—a collection of smaller parts that, when combined, create a whole picture. Break down your goals into smaller, more doable tasks or milestones, and devise a strategy for completing each one.

Staying flexible and adaptable

Life is unpredictable, and things can change in an instant. That's why it's critical to be flexible and adaptable when it comes to goal planning. Be willing to reassess and adapt your goals as needed due to changes in your financial status, priorities, or outside events outside your control.

To maintain concentration and clarity in the middle of life's ever-changing landscape, I devised a goal hierarchy—a prioritized list of objectives based on their importance and urgency. This hierarchy acted as a guidepost, allowing me to allocate resources and prioritize actions based on what was most important at any given time.

By breaking down major goals into smaller, more doable tasks or milestones, I was able to keep up the momentum and track my progress. Each milestone completed acted as a source of motivation and encouragement, driving my drive to keep working toward my ultimate financial goals.

Celebrating Milestones and Progress.

Finally, remember to recognize your accomplishments and improvements along the road. Achieving financial goals requires time, effort, and devotion, so make sure to recognize and reward yourself for your efforts and accomplishments. Celebrating your achievement, whether it's by indulging in a small treat or simply reflecting on how far you've come, will help keep you motivated and inspired to pursue your financial goals.

Conclusion: Empowerment through Goal Setting.

Finally, defining financial objectives is an effective way to achieve financial success and realize your dreams. You can establish a roadmap to attaining your financial objectives by using the SMART approach, prioritizing your goals, creating a goal hierarchy, breaking goals down into achievable steps, remaining flexible and adaptive, and celebrating your milestones and success. So, take the time to dream big, set goals that inspire and encourage you, and then get out there and make them happen. Your financial future is in your control; now grasp it!

Chapter 2. Mastering Money Management: Tracking Expenses and Income.

Mastering money management is similar to arranging a symphony in the complex dance of personal finance, with each note meticulously written and harmonized to produce a melody of financial stability and wealth. The art of recording spending and revenue is important to efficient money management, and it serves as the foundation for sound financial decision-making. In this chapter, we'll look at practical tactics and personal experiences that will help you take charge of your finances and reach your financial goals.

Importance of Tracking Expenses and Income

Consider this scenario: you're sailing a ship into uncharted waters, relying exclusively on instinct and intuition to manage the perilous seas. Without a map or compass to guide you, you're vulnerable to unpredictable currents and fluctuating winds. Consider the same scenario with a precise map and a dependable compass in hand: the voyage becomes smoother, more predictable, and ultimately more successful.

Tracking expenses and income acts as a financial map and compass, providing clarity, insight, and guidance on your path to financial well-being. Understanding where your money comes from and where it goes provides essential insights into your spending patterns, allowing you to find areas for improvement and make informed decisions about how to best manage your resources.

Practical Strategies for Tracking Expenses and Income.

Now that we've discussed the significance of tracking costs and income, let's look at some practical techniques to help you master this crucial skill:

1. Choose your tracking method.

There are numerous techniques for tracking spending and income, ranging from traditional pen and paper to sophisticated budgeting apps and software. Choose a strategy that is appropriate for your interests, lifestyle, and level of technological comfort. Whether you use a simple spreadsheet, a dedicated budgeting program like Mint or YNAB, or a combination of the two, the goal is to find a strategy that works for you and keep to it regularly.

2. Record each transaction.

Every transaction, no matter how minor, must be recorded to ensure effective expense tracking. Make it a habit to record every purchase, payment, and deposit as soon as they occur. This real-time approach provides accuracy and completeness in your spending tracking, reducing the possibility of missing or forgetting crucial transactions.

3. Categorize your expenses.

Categorize your expenses based on your spending habits and priorities. Common categories include accommodation, transportation, groceries, eating out, entertainment, utilities, and savings. Categorizing your spending allows you to see where your money is going and identify areas for potential savings or optimization.

4. Review and analyze your spending patterns.

Review and evaluate your spending patterns regularly to uncover trends, outliers, and areas for improvement. Look for places where you're spending more or less than you should based on your budget or financial goals. Ask yourself why particular expenses are higher or lower than planned, and whether adjustments are required to match your goals.

5. Create realistic budgets and goals.

Create realistic budgets and targets for each expense area based on your spending habits and financial ambitions. Be honest with yourself about how much you can spend, and prioritize expenses that are necessary or consistent with your values and priorities. Set specific spending or savings goals in each category, and track your progress over time.

Overcoming Common Pitfalls.

While tracking costs and income has many advantages, it is not without obstacles and risks. Here are some frequent hurdles you might face along the journey, along with ways to overcome them:

1. Lack of consistency.

Maintaining consistency over time is one of the most difficult aspects of budgeting and tracking money. It's easy to slip into the trap of irregular tracking, in which you note costs or revenue on occasion but don't keep a constant record of your financial transactions. This irregularity might cause gaps in your financial records, making it harder to fully evaluate your spending habits and discover areas for improvement. Without a complete and up-to-date picture of your finances, you may struggle to stay on budget and meet your financial objectives.

Maintaining consistency over time is one of the most difficult aspects of budgeting and tracking money. It's easy to slip into the trap of irregular tracking, where you only record transactions on occasion or neglect to track certain spending completely. To address this difficulty, create a routine and schedule devoted time each day or week to update your spending monitoring system. Consider incorporating monitoring into your daily habits, such as documenting costs before bed or checking your budget with your morning coffee. By making tracking a part of your daily practice, you can ensure that your financial records are consistent and accurate.

2. Difficulty categorizing expenses.

Another prevalent issue is the difficulty of appropriately categorizing expenses. Some expenses may fall into numerous categories, whereas others may not cleanly fit into any specified categories in your monitoring system. To address this issue, use a flexible approach to categorization and be open to making changes as necessary. Consider developing custom categories or subcategories to track unique or irregular spending that do not fit neatly into current categories. Review and modify your classification system on a regular basis to ensure that it is still relevant and matches your evolving spending habits.

3. Overcome Tracking Fatigue

Tracking spending and revenue can be laborious and intimidating, especially when dealing with a high number of transactions or complicated financial conditions. It's easy to become fatigued with tracking and give up entirely. To avoid monitoring fatigue, streamline your tracking procedure and concentrate on the essentials. Prioritize tracking high-value or recurrent spending while remaining conscious of minor transactions that may have little impact on your overall financial picture. Consider automating tracking whenever possible, such as setting up automatic transaction categorization or connecting accounts with budgeting tools, to make the process easier. Remember that even faulty tracking is preferable than no tracking at all, so don't be disheartened by minor lapses or mistakes.

Leveraging Technology for Enhanced Tracking

In today's digital age, technology provides a multitude of tools and services to help you track your expenses more effectively. There are numerous choices for streamlining and automating your tracking process, including budgeting apps and personal financial tools. Investigate several tools and choose the ones that best meet your needs and tastes. Look for tools that simplify and improve your tracking experience, such as automatic transaction categorization, customized budgeting categories, and real-time spending tracking. You may have more control over your spending by utilizing technology to improve your expense tracking.

Conclusion: Empowerment through the tracking of expenses and income.

To summarize, mastering money management begins with the simple skill of recording spending and earning. Understanding where your money comes from and where it goes provides essential insights into your spending patterns, allowing you to find areas for improvement and make informed decisions about how to best manage your resources. You may use monitoring to reach your financial objectives and pave the way to a stronger financial future by employing realistic techniques, personalized anecdotes, and a willingness to overcome obstacles.

Chapter 2: Developing Smart Spending Habits.

In the grand scheme of personal finance, building wise spending habits is analogous to threading a thread of financial wisdom and caution through the fabric of daily life. While the attraction of impulse purchases and rapid gratification may entice us at any time, developing disciplined and conscious spending habits is critical for long-term financial success. In this chapter, we'll look at the art of smart spending, including methods, mindset shifts, and practical advice to help you make sound financial decisions and live within your means.

The Essence of Smart Spending.

Consider walking through a crowded marketplace, surrounded by an overwhelming number of items and services clamouring for your attention. In the middle of this sensory deluge, wise spending acts as a compass, directing you toward purchases that reflect your beliefs, priorities, and financial goals. Smart spending is fundamentally about making deliberate decisions with your money, prioritizing needs over wants, and maximizing the value you get out of every dollar spent.

Strategies for Smart Spending

1. Establish a budget.

Budgeting is fundamental to sensible spending. A budget is your financial road map, providing clarity and direction on how to manage your money between necessary costs, savings goals, and discretionary spending. Begin by documenting your income and expenses, and then develop a budget that matches your financial objectives and goals. Be sure to examine and update your budget frequently to reflect changes in your financial condition or aspirations.

2. Differentiate between needs and wants.

One of the most important concepts of smart spending is distinguishing between needs and wants. Needs are expenses required for survival and well-being, such as food, shelter, and medical care. Wants, on the other hand, are non-essential indulgences that improve our quality of life but are not absolutely necessary. Prioritizing needs over wants in your spending selections ensures that your financial resources are devoted to the most important things.

3. Practice delayed gratification.

In an age of instant pleasure, practicing delayed gratification is an effective approach to developing good spending habits. Instead of succumbing to impulsive inclinations to buy now and pay later, take a step back and consider whether the purchase is consistent with your long-term goals and values. Allow yourself time to examine the advantages and downsides, investigate alternatives, and decide if the purchase is genuinely worthwhile.

4. Comparison Shop

Before making a purchase, compare prices and consider your options. Investigate several brands, sellers, and pricing models to ensure you're getting the best deal for your money. Look for deals, discounts, and promotions, and consider purchasing used or refurbished things when possible. Being a knowledgeable shopper allows you to stretch your budget and make more educated shopping decisions.

5. Set spending limits.

Another successful technique for wise spending is to establish spending limitations or boundaries for various types of expenses. Setting clear parameters for how much you're prepared to spend on groceries, dining out, entertainment, and other discretionary items will help you stick to your budget and avoid overpaying. Consider using cash envelopes or budgeting apps to track your spending in real-time and receive alerts when you're approaching your budget.

6. Embrace minimalism.

In a culture that values luxury and consumption, adopting minimalism is a radical act of disobedience. Minimalism encourages us to simplify our lives, value experiences above goods, and concentrate on what actually offers us joy and contentment. Adopting a minimalist attitude allows you to break free from the shackles of materialism and live more consciously, spending your money on things that are important to you.

Overcoming Common Challenges.

While the road to smart spending is paved with good intentions, it is not without difficulties and barriers. Here are some frequent problems you may face on your route to wise spending, along with suggestions for overcoming them:

1. Peer Pressure

In a culture where social standing and peer approbation are frequently determined by material things, peer pressure may be a potent motivator for excessive spending. To cope with peer pressure, develop a strong sense of self-awareness and confidence in your values and priorities. Surround yourself with people who share your financial objectives and desires, and don't be afraid to set boundaries and say no to unnecessary spending.

2. Emotional Spending

Emotional shopping, or adopting retail therapy to deal with stress, worry, or other emotional issues, can disrupt even the most diligent budgeting efforts. To overcome emotional spending, cultivate self-awareness and mindfulness in your spending behaviours. Before making a purchase, consider whether you're buying out of actual need or to fill an emotional hole. Find healthy ways to deal with underlying feelings, such as practicing self-care, receiving assistance from friends or loved ones, or indulging in hobbies or activities that make you happy without breaking the wallet.

3. Lifestyle Inflation

As your income rises, it's easy to succumb to lifestyle inflation—the tendency to increase your spending in lockstep with your profits. To avoid lifestyle inflation, resist the temptation to update your lifestyle if you obtain a raise or unexpected cash. Instead, prioritize maintaining or even lowering your expenses while boosting your savings and assets. Set specific financial goals and priorities, and devote any additional income to accomplishing them rather than indulging in frivolous indulgences.

4. Impulse purchases.

Impulse purchases are the Achilles' heel of prudent spending, tempting us with promises of rapid delight and transient happiness. To avoid impulse purchases, set a cooling-off period before making any non-essential purchases. Take a step back and give yourself time to analyse whether the buy fits within your budget and priorities. Consider whether you genuinely require the thing or if it is merely a temporary desire. By creating a barrier between impulse and action, you may make more intentional purchasing decisions.

Leveraging Rewards and Incentives.

While smart spending frequently entails cutting back on unnecessary purchases, it is also critical to take advantage of prizes and incentives that can help you stretch your money further. There are several ways to save money and receive rewards on ordinary purchases, including cashback credit cards, loyalty programs, and discount coupons. Make sure to investigate and compare various prizes.

Look for plans that provide the best value while also matching your spending habits and preferences. Just be careful not to let rewards entice you into overspending or making frivolous purchases in search of points or advantages.

Conclusion: A Journey Toward Financial Freedom

Real-Life Strategies for Budget Success

To summarize, building smart spending habits is a transformative process that allows us to gain control of our resources, prioritize our ideals, and live more consciously. By creating a budget, distinguishing between needs and wants, practicing delayed gratification, comparison shopping, setting spending limits, embracing minimalism, and overcoming common obstacles, we can cultivate a mindful consumption mindset and make better financial decisions that align with our long-term goals and aspirations.

Chapter 2: Strategies for Saving and Cutting Costs

In the big symphony of personal finance, saving and decreasing costs are the virtuoso performers who orchestrate financial stability and prosperity. Whether you want to establish an emergency fund, save for a down payment on a house, or achieve financial independence, learning the art of saving and minimizing costs is critical to reaching your financial objectives. In this chapter, we'll look at a variety of practical techniques and concrete recommendations that will help you save more, spend less, and make the most of every dollar.

The Significance of Saving and Cutting Costs

Consider your financial goals to be towering mountains on the horizon, each representing a significant milestone in your path to financial achievement. Saving and decreasing expenditures are the solid boots that take you up the mountain, step by step, bringing you closer to your goal with each economical decision and sensible choice. Whether you're aiming for debt payback, wealth accumulation, or early retirement, saving and decreasing

Real-Life Strategies for Budget Success

spending are the twin foundations that will help you reach your financial goals.

Strategies to Save More

1. Pay Yourself First.

One of the most efficient ways to save more is to "pay yourself first." Treat your savings as a non-negotiable item and set aside a portion of your income for savings before paying for other obligations. Set up automated transfers from your checking account to your savings account once a month to ensure constant and disciplined savings. Prioritizing savings as a top financial priority will help you develop a strong financial foundation and make consistent progress toward your goals.

2. Set specific savings goals.

To keep motivated and focused on your savings efforts, define precise savings goals that correspond to your financial goals. Whether you're saving for an emergency fund, a vacation, a new car, or retirement, having clear and quantifiable goals provides you with a target to shoot for and a path to follow. Divide larger savings goals into smaller, more attainable milestones, and celebrate your accomplishments along the way. By visualizing your goals and measuring your progress, you'll stay inspired and committed to meeting your savings targets.

3. Automate your savings.

Use technology to automate your savings and make them easier. Set up automatic transfers from your checking account to your savings account at regular intervals, such as payday or the first of the month. Consider participating in employer-sponsored retirement plans, such as 401(k)s or IRAs, and contributing automatically through payroll deductions. By automating your savings, you eliminate the temptation to spend money impulsively while also ensuring that your savings grow regularly over time.

4. Reduce unnecessary expenses.

Identify areas where you can cut unneeded costs and redirect the income to savings. Examine your monthly spending and seek for ongoing subscriptions, memberships, or services that you no longer use or require. Cancel or reduce these expenses to free up additional funds for savings. Evaluate your discretionary spending patterns and discover areas where you might save money without sacrificing quality of life. Being careful of your expenditures and making conscientious choices will allow you to save more money.

5. Take advantage of windfalls and bonuses.

When you receive unexpected windfalls or bonuses, such as tax refunds, work bonuses, or monetary presents, fight the inclination to spend them and instead utilize them to increase your savings. Consider putting a percentage of your windfall income into your savings goals, such as creating an emergency fund, paying off debt, or investing for the future. By viewing windfalls as a chance to accelerate your savings progress, you will make considerable headway toward meeting your financial goals sooner.

Strategies for reducing costs

1. Reduce housing expenses.

For many individuals and families, housing bills are among the greatest monthly expenses. Consider downsizing to a smaller, more inexpensive home or apartment, or look into other housing possibilities like renting a room or living with roommates to split costs. Look for ways to negotiate cheaper rent or refinance to further cut your home expenses.

2. Lower utility bills.

Take action to reduce your utility bills and conserve energy to save money on electricity, water, and heating. To save energy, consider investing in energy-efficient appliances, LED light bulbs, and smart thermostats. To save money on your water bill, practice water-saving behaviours like taking shorter showers, replacing leaky faucets, and adopting water-efficient fixtures. Consider combining services and switching to cheaper

Providers for internet, cable, and phone services might further cut your monthly expenses.

3. Reduce Transportation Costs.

Transportation costs can rapidly pile up, especially if you use a car for everyday travel. Consider alternatives to having a car, such as carpooling, biking, walking, or taking public transportation, to save money on petrol, insurance, and maintenance. When having a car is unnecessary, consider ridesharing or rental options for infrequent journeys. If you own a car, keep it in good condition, drive safely, and shop around for the best insurance rates to reduce your transportation costs.

4. Shop Smart.

To save money on everyday purchases, shop strategically and intentionally. Use sales, discounts, and coupons to save money on groceries, household supplies, and other necessities. To save money on groceries without sacrificing quality, go for generic or store-brand products rather than name brands. Plan your meals and make a grocery list before going shopping to avoid impulse purchases and reduce food waste. Consider buying in bulk or joining a warehouse club to save money on commonly used items.

5. Reduce Dining and Entertainment Expenses.

Dining out and entertainment bills can easily deplete your budget if left uncontrolled. Limit dining out to special occasions or infrequent indulgences, and instead cook at home as a more cost-effective option. Explore free or low-cost entertainment choices such as outdoor activities, community events, and DIY projects to spend your leisure time without breaking the bank. Look for discounts or specials on dining and entertainment activities to save money without losing fun.

Overcoming Common Challenges.

Saving and lowering costs have several advantages, but they are not without problems and obstacles. Here are some common problems you may meet on your route to financial freedom, along with ways to overcome them:

1. Lifestyle Inflation

As your income rises, it's easy to succumb to lifestyle inflation—the tendency to increase your spending in lockstep with your profits. To avoid lifestyle inflation, resist the temptation to update your lifestyle if you obtain a raise or unexpected cash. Instead, prioritize maintaining or even lowering your expenses while boosting your savings and assets. Set specific financial goals and priorities, and devote any additional income to accomplishing them rather than indulging in frivolous indulgences.

2. Peer Pressure

In a culture where social standing and peer approbation are frequently determined by material things, peer pressure may be a potent motivator for excessive spending. To cope with peer pressure, develop a strong sense of self-awareness and confidence in your values and priorities. Surround yourself with people who share your financial objectives and desires, and don't be afraid to set boundaries and say no to unnecessary spending.

3. Emotional Spending

Emotional shopping, or adopting retail therapy to deal with stress, worry, or other emotional issues, can disrupt even the most diligent budgeting efforts. To overcome emotional spending, cultivate self-awareness and mindfulness in your spending behaviors. Before making a purchase, consider whether you're buying out of actual need or to fill an emotional hole. Find healthy ways to deal with underlying feelings, such as practicing self-care, receiving assistance from friends or loved ones, or indulging in hobbies or activities that make you happy without breaking the wallet.

4. Lack of financial literacy

A lack of financial awareness can limit your ability to save and cut spending effectively. Take the time to learn about personal finance fundamentals, budgeting strategies, and money-saving techniques. To broaden your knowledge and skills, look for credible information sources such as books, articles, podcasts, and online courses. Consider working with a financial advisor or coach to create a personalized financial plan and receive help based on your specific needs and goals.

Conclusion: A Path to Financial Freedom.

To summarize, learning the skill of saving and lowering costs is a transforming path that allows us to gain control of our resources, prioritize our goals, and live more consciously. By implementing tactics for saving more, decreasing spending, and overcoming frequent problems, we may lay a firm financial foundation and make consistent progress toward our long-term goals. So embrace the trip, stay focused on your goals, and approach each step with purpose and dedication. Your financial future is within reach; begin building it today.

Chapter: Maximizing Income Potential; Exploring Additional Income Streams

In the intricate dance of personal finance, maximizing income potential is akin to unlocking a hidden treasure trove of opportunities, each offering the promise of greater financial security and prosperity. Whether you're striving to pay off debt, build wealth, or achieve financial independence, diversifying your income streams and exploring new avenues for earning can significantly impact your financial trajectory. In this chapter, we'll embark on a journey of discovery, exploring the myriad ways to maximize your income potential and unlock new pathways to financial success.

The Power of Multiple Income Streams

Imagine your income as a mighty river, flowing steadily towards the sea of financial stability and abundance. Now imagine channelling that river into multiple streams, each contributing its own tributary to the flow of wealth and prosperity. This is the power of multiple income streams—a diversified portfolio of earnings that offers resilience, flexibility, and the potential for exponential growth. By diversifying your income sources, you not only increase your earning potential but also mitigate the risks associated with relying on a single source of income.

Strategies for Exploring Additional Income Streams

1. Identify Your Skills and Interests

Begin by identifying your skills, talents, and interests—the unique strengths and passions that set you apart. Consider your professional experience, educational background, hobbies, and areas of expertise. What skills do you possess that are in demand in the marketplace? What activities do you enjoy doing in your spare time? By aligning your income-generating activities with your skills and interests, you'll not only enjoy greater fulfilment but also increase your chances of success.

2. Explore Freelancing and Consulting

Freelancing and consulting offer flexible and lucrative opportunities to leverage your skills and expertise on a project basis. Whether you're a writer, designer, programmer, marketer, or consultant, there's a high demand for freelance talent in virtually every industry. Explore online platforms such as Upwork, Freelancer, and Fiverr to find freelance gigs and connect with clients. Consider offering your services as a consultant to businesses or individuals seeking expert advice and guidance in your field.

3. Start a Side Business

Starting a side business is another effective way to explore additional income streams and pursue your entrepreneurial aspirations. Identify a niche or market opportunity that aligns with your interests and expertise, and develop a product or service to address a need or solve a problem. Launch an online store, create digital products, offer online courses or coaching services, or start a blog or YouTube channel to monetize your knowledge and skills. With the rise of e-commerce platforms and digital marketing tools, starting a side business has never been more accessible or affordable.

4. Invest in Real Estate

Investing in real estate is a time-tested strategy for generating passive income and building long-term wealth. Consider purchasing rental properties, either residential or commercial, and renting them out to tenants to generate rental income. Alternatively, explore real estate crowdfunding platforms or real estate investment trusts (REITs) to invest in real estate without the hassle of property management. With careful research and due diligence, real estate can be a lucrative income stream that provides steady cash flow and capital appreciation over time.

5. Invest in Dividend-Paying Stocks

Investing in dividend-paying stocks is another popular strategy for generating passive income and building wealth over time. Dividend-paying stocks are companies that distribute a portion of their earnings to shareholders in the form of dividends. By investing in dividend-paying stocks, you can earn regular income from dividend payments while potentially benefiting from capital appreciation as the stock price increases. Look for companies with a track record of consistent dividend payments and a strong financial position to maximize your income potential.

6. Explore Affiliate Marketing

Affiliate marketing offers a low-risk, high-reward opportunity to earn passive income by promoting products or services and earning a commission for each sale or lead generated. Join affiliate programs offered by companies in your niche or industry and promote their products or services through your website, blog, social media channels, or email list. Choose products or services that align with your audience's interests and needs, and provide valuable content and recommendations to drive traffic and conversions. With the right strategy and approach, affiliate marketing can be a lucrative income stream that complements your existing revenue streams.

Overcoming Common Challenges

While exploring additional income streams offers numerous benefits, it's not without its challenges and obstacles. Here are some common challenges you may encounter on your journey toward maximizing your income potential and strategies for overcoming them:

1. Time Management

Balancing multiple income streams requires effective time management and prioritization of tasks. To overcome time management challenges, create a schedule or calendar to allocate time to each income-generating activity based on its importance and urgency. Set boundaries and limits on your time to prevent burnout and ensure a healthy work-life balance. Consider outsourcing or delegating tasks that can be handled by others to free up more time for income-generating activities.

2. Skill Development

Exploring new income streams often requires acquiring new skills or expanding your existing skill set. To overcome skill development challenges, invest in ongoing learning and professional development opportunities. Take online courses, attend workshops or seminars, read books, and seek out mentors or experts in your field for guidance and advice. Focus on acquiring skills that are in demand in the marketplace and align with your income-generating goals.

3. Financial Risk

Venturing into new income streams carries inherent financial risks, including start-up costs, investment capital, and potential losses. To mitigate financial risk, conduct thorough research and due diligence before committing to any new income-generating opportunity. Start small and test the waters before scaling up your efforts. Diversify your investments and income streams to spread risk across different asset classes and industries. Consider setting aside an emergency fund to cover unexpected expenses or income fluctuations and protect your financial security.

4. Market Saturation

Entering crowded or competitive markets can pose challenges for new income streams, as you'll be competing with established players and incumbents for market share and customers. To overcome market saturation challenges, differentiate yourself by offering unique products or services, targeting niche markets or underserved audiences, or providing superior quality, value, or customer service. Focus on building and providing solutions to their pain points or needs that set you apart from the competition.

Conclusion: Unlocking Your Income Potential

In conclusion, exploring additional income streams is a transformative journey that empowers us to maximize our earning potential, diversify our income sources, and unlock new pathways to financial success. By identifying our skills and interests, exploring freelancing, consulting, starting a side business, investing in real estate and stocks, and exploring affiliate marketing, we can create a diversified portfolio of income streams that provides resilience, flexibility, and the potential for exponential growth.

Chapter 3: Maximizing Income Potential

In the pursuit of financial freedom and security, maximizing income potential stands as a pivotal pillar of success. While managing expenses and saving diligently are crucial components of sound financial management, increasing your income offers an equally powerful avenue for achieving your financial goals. In this chapter, we'll delve into practical strategies and actionable steps to unlock your earning potential, allowing you to pave the way toward a brighter and more prosperous future.

The Significance of Maximizing Income Potential

Imagine your income as a river, flowing steadily through the landscape of your life. Now picture that river widening and deepening, branching off into tributaries that nourish and sustain you from multiple directions. This is the essence of maximizing income potential—a journey of expansion and abundance that opens doors to new opportunities and possibilities. By harnessing the power of income generation, you not only enhance your financial security but also gain the freedom to pursue your passions, support your loved ones, and make a meaningful impact in the world.

Strategies for Maximizing Income Potential

1. Invest in Education and Skill Development

Investing in education and skill development is one of the most effective ways to increase your income potential. Identify areas where you can enhance your knowledge and expertise, whether through formal education, professional certifications, or self-study. Consider pursuing advanced degrees, attending workshops or seminars, or enrolling in online courses to develop new skills or deepen existing ones. By continuously investing in your personal and professional growth, you'll position yourself for career advancement, higher-paying opportunities, and increased earning potential.

2. Pursue Career Advancement Opportunities

Advancing your career is another effective strategy for maximizing income potential. Take proactive steps to position yourself for advancement within your current company or industry, such as seeking out leadership roles, volunteering for challenging projects, or pursuing additional responsibilities. Update your resume and LinkedIn profile to highlight your achievements and skills, and actively network with colleagues and industry professionals to explore new opportunities. By demonstrating your value and ambition, you'll increase your chances of securing promotions, salary increases, and other career advancement opportunities.

3. Explore Side Hustles and Freelancing

Side hustles and freelancing offer flexible and lucrative opportunities to supplement your primary income and increase your overall earning potential. Identify your skills, interests, and passions, and explore ways to monetize them through freelancing, consulting, or starting a side business. Consider offering your services on freelance platforms like Upwork, Fiverr, or Freelancer, or launching your own business venture based on your unique talents and expertise. By diversifying your income streams and exploring new avenues for earning, you'll create additional opportunities to increase your overall income and financial stability.

4. Negotiate Your Salary and Benefits

Negotiating your salary and benefits is a critical step in maximizing your income potential and ensuring you're fairly compensated for your contributions. Research industry salary benchmarks and comparable positions to determine your market value, and use this information to advocate for a higher salary during job interviews or performance reviews. Be prepared to articulate your achievements, skills, and qualifications, and make a compelling case for why you deserve to be paid more. Additionally, consider negotiating other aspects of your compensation package, such as bonuses, stock options, and benefits, to maximize your overall compensation.

5. Monetize Your Passions and Hobbies

Monetizing your passions and hobbies is a creative and fulfilling way to increase your income potential while doing what you love. Identify activities or interests that bring you joy and fulfilment, whether it's photography, writing, crafting, or gardening, and explore ways to monetize them through freelance work, teaching, or selling products or services. Consider launching a blog or

Real-Life Strategies for Budget Success

YouTube channel to share your expertise and attract an audience, or selling handmade goods or digital products online. By turning your passions into profit, you'll not only increase your income potential but also find greater fulfilment and satisfaction in your work.

Overcoming Encounters

While maximizing income potential offers numerous benefits, it's not without its challenges and obstacles. Here are some common challenges you may encounter on your journey toward increasing your income potential and strategies for overcoming them:

1. Lack of Confidence

A lack of confidence can hold you back from advocating for yourself, pursuing new opportunities, and realizing your full earning potential. To overcome this challenge, focus on building your self-esteem and self-assurance through positive self-talk, affirmations, and visualization techniques. Surround yourself with supportive friends, family members, and mentors who believe in your abilities and encourage you to reach your goals. Practice stepping out of your comfort zone and taking calculated risks to build your confidence and expand your horizons.

2. Time Constraints

Balancing multiple responsibilities and commitments can be challenging, especially when pursuing additional income streams on top of your primary job or family obligations. To overcome time constraints, prioritize your tasks and activities based on their importance and urgency, and allocate time to income-generating activities each day or week. Streamline your workflow and eliminate time-wasting activities to make the most of your available time. Consider outsourcing or delegating tasks that can be handled by others to free up more time for income-generating activities.

3. Fear of Failure

The fear of failure can be a significant barrier to exploring new income opportunities and taking risks in pursuit of your goals. To overcome this fear, reframe failure as a learning opportunity and a natural part of the growth process. Embrace a growth mindset that views setbacks and challenges as opportunities for growth and improvement. Break down your goals into smaller, more manageable steps, and celebrate your progress along the

Real-Life Strategies for Budget Success

way. Surround yourself with supportive individuals who encourage you to take risks and pursue your dreams, even in the face of uncertainty.

Challenge:

Identify one goal or opportunity that you've been hesitant to pursue due to fear of failure. Break down this goal into smaller, more manageable steps, and create a plan for how you'll overcome any obstacles or challenges along the way. Take the first step towards pursuing this goal today, and remind yourself that failure is simply a stepping stone on the path to success.

4. Financial Constraints

Financial constraints can limit your ability to invest in education, pursue career advancement opportunities, or explore new income streams. To overcome this challenge, focus on maximizing your resources and leveraging opportunities for growth and advancement. Look for scholarships, grants, or financial aid programs that can help offset the cost of education or training. Seek out free or low-cost resources for skill development, such as online courses, workshops, or networking events. Be proactive in seeking out opportunities for career advancement within your current organization or industry, and consider negotiating for higher compensation or benefits to improve your financial situation.

Conclusion: Embracing the Journey to Financial Empowerment

In conclusion, maximizing income potential is a transformative journey that empowers you to unlock your full earning capacity, pursue your passions, and create a life of abundance and realisation. By investing in education and skill development, pursuing career advancement opportunities, exploring side hustles and freelancing, negotiating your salary and benefits, and monetizing your passions and hobbies, you'll create multiple avenues for increasing your income and achieving your financial goals. So take a grip of the journey, face challenges with courage and resilience, and seize the opportunities that await you on the path to financial empowerment.

Real-Life Strategies for Budget Success

Chapter 3: Making the Most of Your Resources

In the quest for financial independence and prosperity, the ability to make the most of your resources is a fundamental skill that can pave the way for success. Whether it's time, money, skills, or opportunities, maximizing your resources allows you to achieve more with less, unlocking new pathways to growth and abundance. In this chapter, we'll explore practical strategies and actionable steps to help you leverage your resources effectively, empowering you to build a brighter and more prosperous future.

The Value of Resourcefulness

Resourcefulness is the art of making the most of what you have, whether it's time, money, skills, or connections. It's about finding creative solutions to challenges, seizing opportunities, and maximizing the impact of your efforts. In a world of finite resources and endless demands, resourcefulness is the secret sauce that sets successful individuals apart from the rest. By cultivating a mindset of resourcefulness, you can overcome obstacles, achieve your goals, and thrive in any environment.

Strategies for Making the Most of Your Resources

1. Budgeting and Financial Planning

Budgeting is the cornerstone of effective resource management, providing a roadmap for how you'll allocate your income and expenses. Start by assessing your current financial situation, including your income, expenses, debts, and savings. Identify areas where you can cut back or reduce expenses, and set realistic goals for saving and investing. Use budgeting tools and apps to track your spending, monitor your progress, and make adjustments as needed. By creating a budget and sticking to it, you'll maximize the impact of your financial resources and achieve your long-term goals faster.

Challenge:

Create a detailed budget for the month ahead, allocating specific amounts to different categories such as groceries, housing, transportation, and entertainment. Track your expenses daily and compare them to your budget to ensure you're staying on track.

2. Time Management

Time is a precious resource that, once spent, cannot be reclaimed. Effective time management is essential for making the most of your time and accomplishing your goals. Start by identifying your priorities and setting clear, achievable objectives for each day, week, and month. Use tools such as calendars, planners, and task lists to organize your schedule and prioritize your tasks. Allocate time for important activities such as work, family, self-care, and personal development, and eliminate or delegate tasks that don't align with your goals. By managing your time effectively, you'll maximize your productivity and achieve more in less time.

Task:

Create a daily schedule or to-do list outlining your tasks and priorities for the day. Allocate specific blocks of time to each task and eliminate distractions to maximize your focus and productivity.

3. Skill Development and Learning

Investing in your skills and knowledge is one of the best ways to maximize your resources and unlock new opportunities for growth and success. Identify areas where you can improve or develop new skills that are in demand in your industry or field. Take advantage of online courses, workshops, seminars, and books to expand your knowledge and expertise. Seek out mentors, coaches, or experts in your field who can provide guidance and support as you pursue your goals. By continually investing in your personal and professional development, you'll enhance your value and effectiveness in the marketplace.

Task:

Identify one skill or area of knowledge that you'd like to develop or improve. Research online courses, books, or resources related to that skill, and commit to dedicating time each day to learn and practice.

4. Networking and Relationship Building

Developing relationships and connections with people is an invaluable resource that can lead to new opportunities and partnerships. Take the time to build your business and personal networks, both online and off. Attend networking events, industry conferences, and social gatherings to meet new people and broaden your contact list. Contact your mentors, peers, and co-workers for guidance, support, and cooperation opportunities. Building great relationships and connections will provide you with significant resources, insights, and chances to help you reach your objectives.

Real-Life Strategies for Budget Success

Daily Test:

Every day, reach out to at least one new contact or connection from your network. Send a personalized email or LinkedIn message introducing yourself and expressing your want to connect or collaborate.

5. Creativity & Innovation

Creativity and innovation are great tools for making the best use of your resources and developing unique solutions to problems. Develop a mindset of inquiry, experimentation, and open-mindedness, and be receptive to new ideas and opinions. Look for ways to look outside the box and tackle problems from new perspectives. Encourage brainstorming and idea development in your personal and professional efforts, and be open to taking chances and trying new approaches. By utilizing the power of creativity and invention, you will discover new possibilities and chances that can revolutionize your life and career.

Daily Challenge Tasks:

Set aside some time each day for creative thinking and brainstorming. Keep a notepad or notebook ready to scribble down ideas, insights, and inspiration as they occur to you.

Overcoming Common Challenges

While optimizing your resources has many advantages, it is not without problems and obstacles. Here are some common problems you may face on your journey, along with ways to overcome them.

1. Procrastination and Inertia

Procrastination and inertia might keep you from taking action and making the best use of your resources. To overcome these obstacles, divide jobs into smaller, more manageable chunks and complete them one at a time. Set deadlines and hold yourself accountable to complete projects on time. To fight procrastination and enhance productivity, use tactics like time blocking, pomodoro sessions, and the two-minute rule.

2. Lack of Focus and Distractions

Distractions and a lack of attention can undermine your efforts to optimize your resources and achieve your objectives. To address these issues, set up a separate workstation free of distractions and interruptions. Turn off notifications on your phone and computer, and schedule times for accessing email and social media. Deep breathing, meditation, and visualization are examples of mindfulness and concentration techniques that can help you focus and attention.

Daily Challenge Tasks:

Identify one distraction or source of procrastination that consistently disturbs your concentration. Setting boundaries, creating time limits, or removing temptation from your environment are all proactive ways to reduce or eliminate distractions

3. Fear of failure and perfectionism.

Fear of failure and perfectionism can prevent you from taking risks and making the most of your resources. To overcome these obstacles, view failure as a natural part of the learning process that provides opportunities for growth and improvement. Embrace an experimental and iterative approach, and be willing to take measured risks and learn from your failures. Set realistic goals for yourself and focus on progress, not perfection.

4. Lack of Support and Accountability

Without assistance and accountability, it can be difficult to keep motivated and focused on utilizing your resources. To overcome this obstacle, seek help from friends, family, or coworkers who share your aims and values. Join online forums, mastermind groups, or accountability partnerships to meet like-minded people and hold one another accountable for progress and achievement.

Conclusion: Empowering Yourself to Thrive.

To summarize, making the most of your resources is a transformative journey that allows you to accomplish more with less, discover new opportunities, and live a life of wealth and accomplishment. By adopting a resourceful mentality, efficiently leveraging your time, money, skills, and relationships, and overcoming common obstacles, you may increase your chances of success and create a brighter future for yourself and others around you.

Chapter 4: Navigating Debt; Understanding Different Types of Debt

Debt. It's a word that has weight and meaning in our financial lives. For some, it is an essential instrument for achieving objectives and gaining assets. Others see it as a burden, limiting their freedom and prospects. In this chapter, we'll take a voyage across debt's complicated environment, looking at its numerous forms, potential problems, and effective management measures.

The Importance of Understanding Debt

Debt is a two-edged sword—a powerful weapon that, when used effectively, may lead to opportunity and wealth; when misused, it can lead to financial difficulty and suffering. Understanding the many types of debt, their consequences, and how to properly handle them is critical for financial well-being and security. By demystifying debt and arming yourself with knowledge and techniques for managing it, you can make informed decisions that are consistent with your goals and values, paving the way for a healthier financial future.

Understanding the Different Types of Debt

1. Good Debt.

Good debt is debt used to finance investments or assets with the potential to grow in value over time. Examples of good debt are:

Student Loans: Education is frequently viewed as an investment in yourself and your future earning potential. Student loans can help finance higher education while also increasing long-term earning capability.

Mortgages: Purchasing a home is one of the largest purchases most people will make in their lifetime. A mortgage allows you to buy a property and gradually increase your equity, perhaps leading to long-term financial stability and wealth growth.

firm Loans: Starting or growing a firm frequently necessitates capital investment. Business loans can provide the cash required to start a new business or expand an existing one, with the potential for high returns on investment.

Real-Life Strategies for Budget Success

Daily Challenge Tasks:

Evaluate your existing debt and classify it as "good" or "bad" debt based on its purpose and possible return on investment. Identify any possibilities to refinance or combine high-interest debt in order to improve your financial position.

2. Bad Debt

Bad debt, on the other hand, is debt that is utilized to fund consumption or lifestyle needs but provides no long-term value or return on investment. Examples of bad debt are:

Credit Card Debt: Using credit cards to cover ordinary costs or luxury goods can result in high-interest debt that builds up quickly and is difficult to repay.

Payday Loans: These are short-term, high-interest loans that are commonly used to meet unforeseen bills or financial emergencies. They frequently charge high fees and can trap debtors in a debt cycle.

Auto Loans: While auto loans may be required to purchase a vehicle, financing a car with a high-interest loan or an extended payback period might result in negative equity and financial distress.

Daily Challenge Tasks:

Examine your credit card statements for any recurrent spending or avoidable purchases that add to credit card debt. Create a plan to decrease or eliminate this spending, and use the savings to pay down your credit card balances. This could include cancelling unnecessary subscriptions, preparing meals instead of eating out, or finding non-monetary methods to engage yourself. Once you've found places where you can cut back, commit to reallocating those monies to your debt reduction strategy. Every dollar saved brings you closer to financial freedom.

Chapter 4: Establishing a Debt Repayment Plan

Debt can feel like a crushing burden, weighing down your finances and restricting your freedom. Whether it's credit card debt, student loans, or medical bills, owing money can be stressful and upsetting. But there is hope. With a clear plan and determination, you can overcome your debt and take control of your financial destiny. In this chapter, we'll look at how to create a debt payback plan that works for you, allowing you to overcome debt and attain financial freedom.

The Importance of Creating a Debt Payment Plan

A debt payback plan functions as a road map to financial independence, providing direction, structure, and incentive as you fight to become debt-free. Without a plan, it is easy to become overwhelmed and confused about where to begin. However, with a strategy in place, you will have a clear path forward, guiding your activities and keeping you focused on your objectives. Whether your debt is huge or small, developing a repayment strategy is the first step toward regaining control of your money and building a better future.

Step 1: Take Inventory of Your Debt

The first step in constructing a debt payback plan is to assess your existing financial status. Gather all of your debt-related statements, bills, and papers, and create a list of each debt you owe. Include the total balance, interest rate, minimum monthly payment, and due date for each debt. This will offer you a clear image of what you're dealing with and where you're at financially.

Step 2: Set your goals.

Once you have a comprehensive grasp of your debts, you can create payback targets. Begin by establishing your ultimate aim. Is it to become debt-free? To pay off a specific debt by a particular date? Or to reduce your total debt load by a specific percentage? Make sure your goal is SMART (specific, measurable, achievable, relevant, and time-bound).

Step 3: Select a Repayment Strategy

There are various ways to repay your debts, each with perks and downsides. Some typical tactics are:

Real-Life Strategies for Budget Success

Debt Snowball: This technique focuses on paying off the smaller debts first while making minimum payments on larger bills. When the smallest debt is paid off, you roll the amount you were paying on it onto the next lowest bill, and so on until all of your debts are paid off.

Debt Avalanche: The debt avalanche approach entails repaying your obligations in the sequence of greatest to lowest interest rate. You make the minimum payments on all of your bills while directing any additional funds to the debt with the highest interest rate. Once that loan is paid off, you proceed to the next highest interest rate debt, and so on.

Debt Consolidation: Debt consolidation entails consolidating several loans into a single loan with a lower interest rate. This can help you manage your debt and potentially save money on interest. However, before going with any consolidation loan, you should carefully analyse the terms and expenses.

Step 4: Set a Budget

A budget is an essential tool for managing your money and adhering to your debt repayment strategy. Begin by noting all of your revenue sources, as well as your fixed and variable expenses. Then, set aside a percentage of your salary for debt repayment, making sure to prioritize your highest-interest debt first.

Step 5: Track Your Progress

Once you've developed your debt repayment strategy, you should monitor your progress regularly to ensure you're on pace to meet your objectives. Keep track of your payments, remaining balances, and interest rates, and alter your plan as necessary to reflect any changes in your financial circumstances.

Step 6: Stay Motivated

Paying off debt can be a lengthy and difficult process, but keeping motivated is essential for success. Find methods to celebrate your accomplishments, whether it's completing a goal in your debt repayment plan or discovering new ways to save money. Surround yourself with supportive friends and family members who can encourage you and hold you accountable. Remember the ultimate goal: financial freedom and a happier future.

Daily Challenge Task:

Today's challenge is to follow the steps indicated above to build a debt repayment plan. Take an inventory of your debts, set goals, select a repayment strategy, build a budget, and monitor your progress. Remember that each step you take puts you closer to financial freedom. You have got this!

Chapter 4: Avoiding Common Debt Traps.

Debt traps lie around every corner, luring us with promises of rapid realisation and simple answers to our financial problems. Credit cards, payday loans, and high-interest financing offers can all entice naive consumers into a cycle of debt and financial difficulty. But do not be afraid! With awareness, education, and a healthy dose of scepticism, you may safely traverse the hazardous waters of consumer debt. In this chapter, we will look at some of the most prevalent debt traps and offer practical solutions for avoiding them.

Understanding Common Debt Traps.

Before we get into how to avoid debt traps, let's look at some of the most common traps that customers fall into:

1. Credit card debt.

Credit cards can be a useful financial tool when used appropriately, allowing you to make purchases, develop credit, and earn points. However, if not managed properly, they might lead to debt. With high interest rates and tempting rewards offers, it's easy to overspend and amass more debt than you can afford to pay off.

2. Payday Loans

Payday loans are short-term, high-interest loans that are frequently utilized to meet unforeseen bills or financial problems. While they may appear to be a quick remedy for cash flow concerns, they are frequently accompanied by high fees and interest rates, trapping borrowers in a debt cycle.

3. Rent-to-Own Stores

Rent-to-own stores allow customers to lease furniture, appliances, electronics, and other items with the expectation of eventual ownership. While this may appear enticing to people with limited cash or credit, the high charges and unfavourable restrictions associated with these agreements can soon build up, leaving customers paying significantly more than the retail price of the items.

4: Buy Now, Pay Later Services

Buy now, pay later services enable customers to make purchases and pay in instalments over time, sometimes with no low-interest financing. While this is useful for budget-conscious buyers, it may also lead to overspending and debt accumulation if not used wisely.

Practical Strategies to Avoid Debt Traps

Now that we've identified some typical debt traps, let's look at practical ways to prevent them and stay financially healthy:

1. Create an Emergency Fund

A well-stocked emergency fund is one of the best ways to avoid debt traps. Having a cash reserve set aside for unexpected needs will help you avoid taking out high-interest loans or incurring credit card debt when emergencies strike. Aim to save three to six months' worth of living costs in a readily accessible savings account.

Daily Challenge Task:

Set an emergency fund savings target and plan to attain it. Begin by setting aside a small sum of money each week or month, then gradually increase your contributions as your budget allows. Remember that every dollar saved gets you one step closer to financial security.

2. Keep to a Budget

Creating and sticking to a budget is critical for avoiding overspending and falling into debt. Begin by documenting your income and expenses, then divide your funds between necessary expenses, savings goals, and debt reduction. Set aside some dollars for discretionary spending, but avoid exceeding your budgeted amounts.

Daily Challenge Task: Review your spending habits and identify areas where you overspend. Create a plan to control your spending in these areas, whether by setting spending limits, seeking lower-cost alternatives, or eliminating non-essential items entirely.

3. Avoid high-interest debt.

High-interest debt, such as credit card debt and payday loans, can quickly become out of hand, trapping you in a debt cycle. Whenever possible, avoid high-interest loans in favour of lower-cost financing choices. If you already have high-interest debt, focus on paying it off as soon as possible to reduce interest payments.

Daily Challenge Task

Pay off high-interest debt first. Consider combining high-interest loans with reduced-interest loans or transferring credit card balances to a card with a lower APR to save money on interest.

4. Read the fine print.

Before signing any financial agreements or contracts, read the fine print and ensure that you understand the terms and circumstances. Pay particular attention to interest rates, fees, fines, and repayment terms, and ask clarifying questions if any are unclear. Don't be scared to shop around and compare offers from several lenders or suppliers to find the greatest bargain.

Trial Challenge:

Take some time to study the terms and conditions of your current financial accounts and agreements, such as credit cards, loans, and leases. Pay close attention to any fees, interest rates, or penalties that may apply, and make a note of any modifications you wish to make to your contracts.

5. Practice Delayed Gratification.

One of the most effective methods to minimize debt is to practice delayed gratification. Instead of giving in to the lure of instant gratification and impulse purchases, take a step back and consider whether the item is genuinely worth the money. Consider setting a waiting period before making any non-essential purchases to provide yourself time to determine whether it is a sensible financial move.

Daily Challenge

Before making non-essential purchases, consider whether the item is genuinely necessary or just a desire. Consider setting a 24-hour waiting period before making any impulse purchases to allow yourself time to assess the benefits and drawbacks.

Conclusion: Empowering Yourself to Avoid Debt Traps.

Avoiding typical debt traps involves diligence, dedication, and a willingness to make sound financial decisions. By creating an emergency fund, sticking to a budget, avoiding high-interest debt, reading the fine language, and practicing delayed gratification, you may protect yourself from the dangers of consumer debt and attain financial health and stability. Remember that every modest step toward financial management puts you closer to a happier, debt-free future.

Chapter 5: Thriving in Daily Life: Budget-Friendly Meal Planning and Cooking Tips.

Food is more than just nutrition; it's an essential aspect of our everyday life. However, the cost of food may quickly build up, putting a strain on our wallets and making it difficult to eat healthily while staying within our budgetary limits. But do not be afraid! With a little ingenuity, preparation, and smart shopping, you can have great, nutritious meals without breaking the bank. In this chapter, we'll look at practical methods and strategies for budget-friendly meal planning and cooking, allowing you to thrive in everyday life while staying within your budget.

The Benefits of Budget-Friendly Meal Planning

Meal planning is a game changer in terms of grocery savings and eating well on a budget. By planning your meals ahead of time, you may avoid impulse purchases, reduce food waste, and make the best use of your ingredients. Furthermore, meal planning helps you streamline your grocery shopping, saving you time and worry at the store. With a well-planned meal plan in place,

Real-Life Strategies for Budget Success

you can eat great, nutritious meals every day without going overboard.

The Personal Touch: My Journey with Cost-Effective Meal Planning

As someone who believes in both financial responsibility and good eating, I've seen first-hand how meal planning may help you achieve both. In the past, I would spend much too much money on food, only to have half of them go to waste as they sat in the back of my refrigerator. However, after incorporating meal planning into my routine, I experienced a greater sense of control over my food budget and a revived pleasure for cooking.

In my early twenties, I was known for my reckless grocery-buying habits. I'd walk through the store's aisles, placing items into my cart without thinking twice, only to discover later that I had no idea what to do with them. My fridge was a graveyard of wilted greens, expired dairy items, and half-used sauces, demonstrating my lack of planning and foresight.

But when I began to manage my finances and focus on my health, I realized I needed to make a change. So I resorted to meal planning to help me cut back on my spending and make more conscious grocery shop purchases. I began by preparing a weekly meal plan, inventorying what I already had on hand, and developing a list of things I needed to purchase. It was a simple yet dramatic change that allowed me to save money, reduce food waste, and eat healthier every day.

Strategies for Budget-Friendly Meal Planning

1. Begin with What You Have

Before you even consider going to the grocery shop, take stock of what you currently have in your pantry, refrigerator, and freezer. Use up any perishable goods that are about to expire, and come up with dinner ideas based on the ingredients you already have on hand. Starting with what you currently have will help you save money while also reducing food waste.

Daily Challenge

List all ingredients in your cupboard, fridge, and freezer. Challenge yourself to plan at least one dinner using just ingredients you currently own, and be creative with your dish ideas.

2. Plan your meals.

After you've taken inventory of your ingredients, it's time to plan your meals for the week. Consider your schedule, food habits, and any upcoming special events. To make your meals more balanced and satisfying, include a variety of protein, veggies, grains, and legumes. Don't forget to plan leftovers and "clean out the fridge" nights to use up any residual ingredients.

Daily Challenge Task: Plan your weekly meals based on your schedule and available ingredients. Use a meal planning template or app to organize your meals and create a shopping list for any ingredients you'll need.

3. Shop Smart.

With your meal plan and shopping list in hand, you'll arrive at the grocery store with a clear strategy. Stick to your list as much as possible to minimize impulsive purchases and extras. Consider shopping at bargain retailers, buying in bulk, and taking advantage of deals and promotions to make your grocery budget go even further.

Daily Challenge

Go grocery shopping with a food plan and list. Stick to your list and avoid impulse purchases. Challenge yourself to identify at least one item on your list that is on sale or discounted.

4. Embrace Batch Cooking.

Batch cooking is a time-saving approach that entails making big amounts of food at once and portioning it for later meals. Cooking in bulk allows you to save time and energy in the kitchen while also ensuring you always have healthy, handmade meals on hand, even on hectic days. Consider batch cooking essentials like rice, beans, grains, soups, stews, and casseroles, then freezing individual portions for later use.

Daily Challenge

Schedule a batch cooking session. Choose one or two recipes that lend themselves to batch cooking, such as chili, soup, or pasta sauce, and make a large batch to portion out and freeze for later use.

5. Be Creative with Leftovers

Real-Life Strategies for Budget Success

Leftovers are a thrifty cook's best friend. Instead of wasting them, be creative and reuse them into new meals. Leftover roasted veggies, for example, can be mixed into salads, soups, or grain bowls, and cooked grains can be made into fried rice or grain salads. Don't be scared to think outside the box and try alternative taste combinations and cooking methods.

Daily Challenge Task

Check your fridge for any leftovers or ingredients that need to be used up. Challenge yourself to find a unique method to repurpose them into a new dinner or dish. Not only can using up leftovers save you money, but it will also help to reduce food waste.

Conclusion: Empowering Yourself to Thrive on a Budget.

Budget-friendly meal planning and preparation do not have to be difficult jobs. With a little forethought, ingenuity, and smart shopping, you can have great, nutritious meals every day without going overboard. You can take control of your food budget and thrive in everyday life by starting with what you have, planning your meals, shopping wisely, embracing batch cooking, and being creative with leftovers.

Chapter 5: Affordable Transportation Solutions

Transportation is a crucial part of our lives, allowing us to navigate our daily routines, commute to work, and visit new places. However, the expenditures of owning and operating a vehicle can be enormous, especially for those on a limited budget. In this chapter, we'll look at practical and economical transportation choices that can help individuals and families get about while staying within their means.

The importance of affordable transportation

Transportation costs can quickly deplete a household's budget, leaving little room for other necessary bills or savings. High gas prices, insurance premiums, maintenance costs, and monthly car loan payments can all add up, causing financial hardship and worry. Individuals might reduce some of this financial stress by looking for low-cost transportation options.

Real-Life Strategies for Budget Success

Personal Journey: Achieving Financial Freedom with Affordable Transportation

Growing up in a small town, driving a car felt like a rite of passage—a symbol of independence and freedom. However, as I approached maturity and faced the difficulties of managing my finances, I rapidly understood that car ownership came at a high cost. From monthly car payments to rising gas prices and unforeseen repair bills, the cost of owning a vehicle was straining my finances.

Determined to find a more economical answer, I began looking into different ways of transportation. I began bicycling to work as a method to save money on petrol, but I quickly discovered the many benefits of cycling—better health, less stress, and a stronger connection with my community. As I adopted biking as my major form of transportation, I discovered that I was not only saving money but also enjoying the ride more than I had in a car.

In addition to biking, I began taking public transportation for longer journeys or when the weather was not cooperating. By acquiring a monthly transit pass and intelligently arranging my trips, I was able to considerably minimize my transportation costs while still arriving at my destination efficiently and economically. These improvements not only allowed me to save more money but also gave me a new sense of freedom and flexibility in my daily life.

Practical Tips for Cost-Effective Transportation Solutions

1. Investigate other modes of transportation.

Biking, walking, and taking public transportation are all fantastic alternatives to having a car and can dramatically save commuting costs. Biking, for example, is not only inexpensive but also beneficial to one's health and the environment. Consider purchasing a nice bike and researching bike-friendly routes in your neighbourhood for your daily commute or errands.

Daily Challenge Test:

Challenge yourself today to bike or walk to one of your locations rather than driving or taking public transportation. Take note of how much money you save on transportation and how you feel after adding physical exercise to your commute.

2. Carpooling and Ridesharing

Pooling resources with friends, co-workers, or neighbours through carpooling or ride-sharing can help spread transportation costs among numerous people, making it cheaper for everyone. Coordinate schedules and destinations with people in your community to share transportation to work, meetings, or social gatherings, lowering gas costs and environmental effects.

3. Utilize public transportation.

Public transportation systems, such as buses, trains, subways, and trams, provide a low-cost and convenient mode of transportation, particularly in cities with well-developed transit networks. Many cities provide reduced fares for students, pensioners, and frequent passengers, as well as monthly or annual passes that enable unlimited public transportation for a set fee.

Daily Task:

Today, plan a public transportation journey to discover a new neighbourhood, see a local site, or run errands. Familiarize yourself with the transport routes and schedules in your area, and take advantage of any discounts or special offers for riders.

4. Optimize Your Vehicle's Use

If you own a car, there are various ways you may use to cut your commuting expenditures while increasing efficiency. Combine errands into a single trip to save time and gasoline. Maintain your vehicle regularly to avoid costly repairs. Drive conservatively to enhance fuel economy. Instead of purchasing a car, consider car-sharing or renting one for short or lengthy trips.

Challenge:

Today, enhance your vehicle's fuel efficiency by practicing eco-driving strategies such as gentle acceleration, maintaining a steady pace, and limiting idle. Monitor your fuel consumption throughout the day and take note of any increases in mileage or gas savings.

5. Embrace Active Transportation

Walking and cycling are not only inexpensive ways of transportation, but they also provide several health benefits such as increased cardiovascular fitness, lower stress levels, and higher mental well-being. Include walking or cycling in your daily routine whenever possible, whether for commuting to work, running errands, or casually exploring your neighbourhood.

Daily Challenge Tasks:

Today, challenge yourself to walk or bike to all of your destinations, including work, errands, and social gatherings. Take note of how you feel physically and mentally after adopting more active transportation into your daily routine, as well as the possible cost savings vs driving or taking public transportation.

Conclusion: Empowering Yourself With Affordable Transportation

Individuals and families looking to save money on transportation can find affordable solutions. Individuals can save money, lessen their environmental effects, and live a more active and meaningful lifestyle by trying out new forms of transportation such as biking, walking, public transportation, carpooling, and ride-sharing. So, take the first step toward inexpensive transportation now and experience the freedom and flexibility that comes with discovering sustainable and cost-effective alternatives to go where you need to go.

Chapter 5: Find Free and Low-Cost Entertainment Options

Entertainment is an important element of our lives since it provides enjoyment, relaxation, and opportunities for socialization and exploration. However, the cost of leisure activities like movies, concerts, and dining out may quickly add up, putting a strain on our finances. In this chapter, we'll look at practical and imaginative ways to uncover free and low-cost entertainment options so you may have fun without breaking the bank.

The Benefits of Free and Low-Cost Entertainment

In today's fast-paced society, it is easy to fall into the trap of believing that entertainment must be pricey in order to be pleasurable. However, some of the most rewarding and memorable experiences in life can be found in simple, low-cost activities that do not necessitate a significant financial investment. By looking for free and low-cost entertainment choices, you may save money, minimize financial stress, and still have a good time with friends and family.

Personal Reflection: My Path to Embracing Low-Cost Entertainment

Growing up in a low-income home taught me the importance of simple joys and thrifty living at a young age. While my friends were out spending money on pricey events and activities, I discovered the delight of finding free and low-cost entertainment options that allowed me to have the same amount of fun without breaking the bank.

One of my best childhood memories is of spending long summer afternoons at the local park with my siblings and friends, playing games, picnicking, and exploring the outdoors. These simple adventures cost nothing, yet they provided hours of amusement and made lasting memories that I treasure to this day.

As I grew older and approached adulthood, I maintained this mindset, looking for free and low-cost entertainment opportunities in my town. Attending free concerts and art exhibitions, as well as hosting potluck dinners and game nights with friends, taught me that there are numerous ways to have fun without spending much money. Through these events, I learnt that true satisfaction is not determined by how much money you spend, but by the quality of your time with others and the memories you make along the way.

Real-Life Strategies for Budget Success

How to Find Free and Low-Cost Entertainment Options

1. Explore your community.

Exploring your local community and making use of existing services and activities is one of the best ways to locate free and low-cost entertainment. Check out community calendars, local newspapers, and event websites to learn about free concerts, festivals, art exhibitions, and other cultural events in your region.

2. Take advantage of nature.

Nature provides an abundance of free entertainment options, ranging from hiking and picnicking to birdwatching and astronomy. Make use of your local parks, nature reserves, and hiking trails to get outside and enjoy activities like hiking, biking, fishing, and wildlife viewing.

Daily Challenge Tasks:

Spend some time today outside, appreciating nature. Take a walk-through a nearby park, cycle along a gorgeous trail, or pack a picnic and eat lunch outside. Take note of how you feel after spending time in nature, as well as how much you like simple outside activities.

3. Host social gatherings

Hosting social parties at home is an affordable way to entertain friends and family. Plan potluck dinners, game evenings, movie marathons, or DIY craft parties where everyone can bring food, drinks, or activities. These events are not only cost-effective, but they also allow for meaningful interactions and shared experiences.

4. Get creative with DIY projects.

DIY projects and crafts are not only a pleasant and gratifying way to spend your time, but they also provide a low-cost kind of entertainment. Whether you enjoy knitting, painting, woodworking, or baking, there are several DIY projects and hobbies to try that involve little investment in materials and equipment.

Real-Life Strategies for Budget Success

5. Make Use of Free Online Resources

The internet provides a wealth of free entertainment possibilities, such as streaming services, podcasts, online courses, and virtual tours. Make use of these free resources to find new interests, skills, and fascinating material.

Daily Challenge Tasks:

Today, look into a new podcast, online course, or virtual tour that interests you. Whether you're learning a new language, touring a museum exhibit, or listening to a thought-provoking podcast, take advantage of the numerous free internet resources accessible to you.

Conclusion: Enjoying the Benefits of Low-Cost Entertainment

Finding free and low-cost entertainment options does not indicate giving up fun or satisfaction; it simply requires being creative and innovative in how you spend your time and money. Exploring your town, connecting with nature, having social gatherings, participating in DIY projects, and making use of free online resources can help you find infinite ways to have fun without breaking your wallet. Challenge yourself to get acquainted with the delight of low-cost entertainment and to appreciate the simple pleasures of life.

Chapter 6: Planning for the Future and Investing Wisely for Long-Term Financial Stability

Long-term financial stability and security require forward-thinking planning. One of the most effective strategies to develop wealth and safeguard your financial future is to invest wisely. In this chapter, we'll look at the benefits of investing, practical tactics for getting started, and daily challenge activities to help you take control of your financial destiny.

Understanding the Value of Investing

Investing is the process of putting money to work in assets such as stocks, bonds, mutual funds, real estate, and other financial instruments in the hope of earning income or gain over time. While investing entails risk, it also has the potential to generate considerable long-term returns, allowing you to build wealth, achieve financial goals, and ensure your financial future.

Real-Life Strategies for Budget Success

Personal Reflection: My Journey to Invest Wisely

I vividly remember the day I got my first pay check from my first job after college. It seemed like a major accomplishment, a step toward financial independence and freedom. However, as I looked at the amount on my salary check, I understood that if I wanted to meet my long-term financial goals, I needed to do more than just save money; I needed to invest it effectively.

At first, the world of investment appeared scary and overwhelming. There were so many options—stocks, bonds, mutual funds, and ETFs—that I had no idea where to begin. However, I was determined to educate myself and take control of my financial future.

I began by reading books, attending seminars, and getting guidance from financial professionals. I learnt the value of diversification, asset allocation, and risk management, and gradually gained the confidence to begin investing. I began slowly, investing a portion of my savings in low-cost index funds and gradually increasing my contribution as my expertise and comfort level improved.

Over time, I realized the value of investing in action. My investments slowly increased in value, providing me with passive income and assisting me in meeting my long-term financial objectives. Today, investment is an essential component of my financial strategy, giving me peace of mind and confidence in my capacity to ensure my financial future.

How to Invest Wisely for Long-Term Financial Stability

1. Start early and be consistent.

One of the most fundamental investing ideas is to begin early and maintain consistency. The sooner you begin investing, the longer your money has to grow due to the force of compounding. Even little donations made on a regular basis can accumulate over time to help you generate significant wealth. Make investing a habit by establishing automatic contributions to your investment accounts and remaining disciplined in your approach.

Daily Test:

Set up automatic contributions to your investment accounts, such as a 401(k), IRA, or brokerage account. Begin with an amount you are comfortable with and commit to making regular payments to your investments. Monitor your progress and recognize your dedication to achieving long-term financial stability.

2. Diversify your investments.

Diversification is an important approach for controlling risk and increasing returns on your financial portfolio. By diversifying your assets across asset classes, industries, and geographic locations, you can mitigate the impact of a single underperforming investment. Diversification can help you manage risk and reward while also protecting your portfolio from market volatility.

Daily Challenge Tasks:

Today, examine your investment portfolio and determine its level of diversification. Identify any sections of your portfolio that may be overly risky or lack diversification, and make any necessary adjustments to obtain a more balanced profile. Consider diversifying your portfolio by adding exposure to several asset classes such as equities, bonds, real estate, and commodities.

3. Invest for the long term.

Investing is a long-term endeavour, and success requires patience and dedication. Avoid attempting to time the market or chase short-term trends, as this can result in bad investing decisions and undue risk. Instead, concentrate on developing a well-diversified portfolio of high-quality investments and staying committed for the long term in order to fully realize the benefits of compound returns.

Diurnal Challenge Tasks:

Today, evaluate your investment approach and determine whether you are investing with a long-term perspective. Remind yourself of your long-term financial goals and the value of remaining disciplined and patient in your investment strategy. Avoid making impulsive investing decisions based on short-term market volatility, and instead focus on your long-term goals.

4. Take advantage of tax-advantaged accounts.

Tax-advantaged accounts, such as 401(k), IRAs, and HSAs, provide significant advantages that can help you maximize your investment returns while minimizing your tax liability. Take advantage of these accounts to save for retirement, healthcare, and other long-term financial objectives while earning tax-deferred or tax-free returns on your investment. Maximize your contributions to these accounts to fully benefit from the tax advantages they provide.

Challenge:

Today, go over your retirement accounts and see if you're maximizing your contributions to take advantage of the tax breaks available. Consider raising your contributions to these accounts to the greatest allowable limit to maximize your tax-deferred or tax-free growth potential and speed up your progress toward your long-term financial objectives.

5. Stay informed and educated.

The world of investing is always changing, and staying informed and educated is key to making sound financial decisions. Take the time to investigate and understand various investment possibilities, methods, and market trends, and seek guidance from reputable financial professionals as needed. Stay up to date on economic news and market developments that may affect your assets, and adjust your investing plan as needed to stay on pace to meet your financial objectives.

Conclusion: Gaining Control of Your Financial Future Through Wise Investing

Investing intelligently is critical for long-term financial stability and security. Starting early, being consistent, diversifying your investments, investing for the long term, taking advantage of tax-advantaged accounts, and staying informed and educated can help you grow wealth, achieve your objectives, and safeguard your future. So push yourself to take control of your financial future today by following these techniques and making prudent investments for long-term success.

Real-Life Strategies for Budget Success

Chapter 6: Planning for the Future; Budgeting for Retirement.

Retirement is a key life milestone that marks the end of a career-focused existence and the beginning of a new era of leisure, discovery, and relaxation. However, establishing a comfortable retirement needs careful planning and preparation, particularly for those on a limited income. In this chapter, we'll look at practical ways to save for retirement on a budget, the value of starting early, and daily challenging activities to help you take charge of your finances.

The Value of Planning for Retirement

Retirement may seem like a distant dream, but it is never too early to begin planning and preparing for your golden years. With the rising cost of living and uncertainty surrounding social security benefits, it is critical to take proactive measures to ensure a financially comfortable retirement. Starting early, making wise financial decisions, and prioritizing savings can help you develop a nest egg that will support you in retirement and bring you peace of mind in the future.

Practical Strategies for Budget-Friendly Retirement

1. Start early and make saving a priority:

The secret to saving for retirement on a budget is to begin early and make it a priority. Because of the power of compounding, even little payments done on a regular basis can accumulate into a substantial nest egg. Make retirement savings a non-negotiable element of your budget, and set up automatic contributions to retirement accounts to ensure that you continuously save for the future.

2. Take advantage of employer-sponsored retirement plans:

Employer-sponsored retirement plans, such as 401(k)s and 403(b)s, provide essential benefits that can help you save for retirement while staying within your budget. Take advantage of these programs if your employer provides them, and contribute as much as you can afford, particularly if your employer matches your contribution. Maximize your contributions to these accounts to fully benefit from the tax breaks and employer-matching contributions they provide.

Daily Challenge Tasks:

Today, go over your employer-sponsored retirement plan options and see if you're making full use of the benefits provided. Consider raising your retirement plan contributions to maximize your savings potential, and take advantage of any company matching contributions available.

3. Investigate Other Retirement Savings Options:

Aside from employer-sponsored retirement plans, there are additional retirement savings choices available to help you plan for retirement on a budget. Consider setting up an individual retirement account (IRA), such as a Traditional or Roth IRA, to augment your employer-sponsored retirement savings. To maximize your savings potential and reduce tax responsibilities in retirement, consider various tax-advantaged savings choices such as health savings accounts (HSAs) and 529 college savings plans.

Daily Challenge Tasks:

Today, examine the various retirement savings alternatives available to you, such as IRAs, HSAs, and 529 college savings plans. Determine which accounts are appropriate for your financial objectives and circumstances, and consider adding additional accounts to diversify your retirement assets and optimize tax benefits.

4. Cut back on expenses and live below your means:

Living below your means is critical for saving for retirement on a budget. Reduce non-essential expenses and cultivate a conservative mindset to increase your savings. Look for ways to cut your housing, transportation, and discretionary spending, then divert those savings toward retirement savings. To favour long-term financial security over short-term enjoyment, adopt a minimalist lifestyle and place a premium on experiences rather than stuff.

5. Stay informed and educated about retirement planning.

Retirement planning is a complex and ever-changing process, so it's critical to be informed and educated on the newest trends, methods, and possibilities. Take the time to investigate and understand various retirement planning themes, such as investment methods, withdrawal techniques, and healthcare considerations, and get guidance from reputable financial professionals as needed. Stay up to date on economic events and market movements that may affect your retirement savings, and adjust your retirement plan as needed to stay on pace to meet your financial objectives.

Test:

Today, set aside time to learn about a new retirement planning topic or method that interests you. Expand your knowledge of retirement planning by reading a book, listening to a podcast, or attending a webinar. Take notes on key findings and practical insights, then apply them to your retirement strategy to improve your financial literacy and decision-making abilities.

Conclusion: Gaining Control Over Your Retirement Future

Preparing for retirement on a budget involves careful preparation, discipline, and commitment, but the benefits outweigh the effort. Starting early, making saving a priority, taking advantage of employer-sponsored retirement plans, exploring other retirement savings options, cutting back on expenses, and staying informed and educated about retirement planning can help you build a nest egg that will support you in retirement and provide peace of mind in the future. So, push yourself to take charge of your retirement future today and begin planning for a safe and joyful retirement on a budget.

Real-Life Strategies for Budget Success

Conclusion: Embracing the Shoestring Lifestyle for Long-Term Financial Freedom

As we near the end of our trip together, it's time to reflect on the lessons we've learnt, the problems we've encountered, and the changes we've gone through. Throughout this book, we've looked at how adopting a shoestring lifestyle might help you achieve long-term financial freedom. We've looked at practical tactics for budgeting, saving, investing, and living frugally, all with the objective of empowering you to take control of your financial destiny and create a better future for yourself and your loved ones.

The shoestring lifestyle is based on a simple but powerful truth: financial freedom is determined by how you choose to manage and leverage the resources at your disposal, not how much money you have. It is about adopting an attitude of abundance rather than lack, empowerment rather than deprivation. It is about realizing that true prosperity is measured not in dollars and cents, but in freedom, fulfilment, and the opportunity to live life on your own terms.

Throughout our voyage, we've heard stories about tenacity, persistence, and triumph over adversity. We've heard from people who overcame seemingly insurmountable obstacles—a job loss, a medical emergency, a pile of debt—and came out stronger, wiser, and more financially secure than ever. Their experiences serve as a reminder that no matter where you are in your financial journey, it is never too late to take charge and design a new course for a better future.

As we conclude this book, I'd want to leave you with a few closing thoughts and reflections:

1. Mindset Matters

One of the most profound lessons we've learnt is the role of mindset in determining our financial reality. Adopting a positive and empowered mentality allows us to overcome hurdles, accept difficulties, and shift our relationship with money from one of fear and scarcity to one of plenty and opportunity.

2. Little moves Lead to Big Results

Achieving long-term financial freedom requires taking little, consistent moves in the correct direction rather than making drastic changes all at once. Whether you set aside a percentage of your pay check for savings, cut back on non-essential costs, or look into new income prospects, every small step you take gets you closer to your goals.

3. Embrace Creativity and Resourcefulness

Living the shoestring lifestyle necessitates a willingness to think outside the box, devise inventive solutions to financial problems, and make the most of the resources at your disposal. There are numerous methods to stretch your dollars and live well on a budget, such as doing your own home repairs, preparing meals at home instead of going out, or finding free or low-cost entertainment choices.

4. Community and Support

Remember that you are not alone in this path. Seek support from friends, family, and online communities that share your aims and values. Surround yourself with good influencers and cheerleaders who will motivate, support, and hold you accountable while you pursue your financial goals.

5. Celebrate Your Successes

Finally, don't forget to acknowledge your accomplishments along the path, no matter how minor. Whether you've reached a savings milestone, paid off a debt, or met a long-term financial goal, take the time to recognize and enjoy your accomplishments. Celebrating your accomplishments not only raises morale and inspiration but also encourages healthy financial habits and behaviors.

As we end this book's final chapter, I'd want to thank you for joining me on this adventure. Whether you're just starting out on your financial journey or have been on it for a while, I hope the ideas, methods, and stories shared in these pages inspire, empower, and equip you with the tools you need to achieve long-term financial freedom.

Remember that the shoestring lifestyle is a journey, not a destination, leading to a better, more secure, and more rewarding future.

www.ingramcontent.com/pod-product-compliance
Lightning Source LLC
Chambersburg PA
CBHW071932210526
45479CB00002B/642